_____
_____

These are the glorious works, Parent of Good,
Almighty, thine this Universal frame,
Thus wondrous fair, thyself how wondrous then!

JOHN MILTON

# TO REMEMBER IS TO LOVE

## A BIRTHDAY BOOK

Compiled and illustrated by
JOAN BERG VICTOR

The C. R. Gibson Company
Norwalk, Connecticut
*Publishers*

Copyright © MCMLXX by
The C. R. Gibson Company, Norwalk, Connecticut
All rights reserved
Printed in the United States of America
Library of Congress Catalog Card Number: 78-110758
SBN 8378-1718-8

O Lord, how manifold are thy works! in wisdom hast thou made them all: the earth is full of thy riches.

>                                         PSALM 104: 24

And why take ye thought for raiment?
Consider the lillies of the field, how
they grow; they toil not, neither do
they spin:
And yet I say unto you, That even
Solomon in all his glory was not
arrayed like one of these.

>                                         MATTHEW 6:28,29

When daffodils begin to peer,
With heigh! the doxy, o'er the dale,
Why, then comes in the sweet o'the year.

>                                         WILLIAM SHAKESPEARE

Now the bright star, day's harbinger
Comes dancing from the East and leads with her
The flow'ry May, who, from her green lap, throws
The yellow cowslip and the pale primrose.

>                                         JOHN MILTON

Flowers have an expression of countenance as much as men or animals. Some seem to smile, some have a sad expression; some are pensive and diffident; others again are plain, honest and upright, like the broad-faced sunflower and the hollyhock.

Henry Ward Beecher

You are welcome as the flowers in May.

Charles Macklin

A milkweed, and a buttercup, and cowslip,
said sweet Mary,
Are growing in my garden-plot, and this I
Call my dairy.

Peter Newell

In emerald tufts, flowers purple, blue and white;
Like sapphire, pearl and rich embroidery, . . .
Fairies use flowers for their charactery.

William Shakespeare

Of odors sweetest
Such as in summer's tide
Fragrance send forth in places,
Fast in their stations,
Joyously o'er the plains,
Blown plants,
Honey-flowing.

    FROM THE EXETER BOOK

I know a bank whereon the wild thyme blows,
Where oxlips and the nodding violet grows,
Quite over-canopied with luscious woodbine,
With sweet musk-roses and with eglantine:
There sleeps Titania sometime of the night,
Lull'd in these flowers with dances and delight.

    WILLIAM SHAKESPEARE

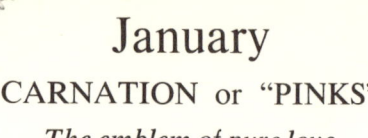

# January
## CARNATION or "PINKS"
*The emblem of pure love*

CARNATION or "coronation" as it was originally spelled, because it was used to make crowns and garlands. It was used as a seasoning for food (thus, it was also called "Gilliflower", its fragrance resembling the spice). It gave tang to liquor (and was known as Sop-in-Wine) and its petals were candied. Writes Gerard: "Conserve made of the flowers of the clove Gilliflower and sugar is exceeding cordial and wonderfully above measure, doth comfort the heart, being eaten now and then."

And I will pu' the pink, the emblem o' my dear,
For she's the pink o' woman kind, and blooms
Without a peer.

>> ROBERT BURNS

To me the meanest flower that blows can give
Thoughts that do often lie too deep for tears.

>> WILLIAM WORDSWORTH

The fairest flowers o' the season
Are our carnations and streak'd gilliflowers.

>> WILLIAM SHAKESPEARE

And still my child-heart quivers with that first ecstacy,
"Carnations are your flower!" my first love says to me!

MARGARET WIDDEMER

# February
## VIOLET

A Woman's love, deep in the heart,
Is like the Violet flower,
That lifts its modest head apart
In some sequestered bower.

        ANONYMOUS

Violet is for faithfulness
Which in me shall abide;
Hoping likewise that from your heart
You will not let it slide

        ANONYMOUS

The Violet . . .
Stands first with most, but always with a lover.

        BARRY CORNWALL

The violets that strew
The green lap of the new-come Spring

        WILLIAM SHAKESPEARE

# March
## DAFFODIL
*The emblem of self-love*

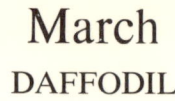

I wandered lonely as a cloud
That floats on high o'er vales and hills,
When all at once I saw a crowd,
A host of golden daffodils,
Beside the Lake, beneath the trees
Fluttering and dancing in the breeze.

Continuous as the stars that shine
And twinkle in the milky way,
They stretched in never-ending line
Along the margin of a bay:
Ten thousand saw I at a glance
Tossing their heads in sprightly dance.

The waves beside them danced, but they
Out-did the sparkling waves in glee:
A poet could not but be gay
In such a jocund company!
I gazed — and gazed — but little thought
What wealth the show to me had brought:

For oft, when on my couch I lie
In vacant or in pensive mood,
They flash upon that inward eye
Which is the bliss of solitude;
And then my heart with pleasure fills,
And dances with the daffodils.

WILLIAM WORDSWORTH

Daffodils
That come before the swallow dares, and take
The winds of March with beauty.

WILLIAM SHAKESPEARE

# April
## DAISY

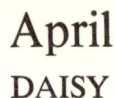

*Symbol of innocence,* true virginity; the English called it "day's eye, the purity, the spring of life." "No doubt it received this designation from its habit of closing its petals at night, which it also does in rainy weather."

L. E. L.

Bright flower, whose home is everywhere!
 Apilgrim bold in Nature's care,
And oft, the long year through, the heir
 Of joy or sorrow;
Methinks that there abides in thee
Some concord with humanity,
Given to no other flower I see
 The forest through!

And wherefore? Man is soon deprest;
A thoughtless thing who once unblest,
Does little on his memory rest,
 Or on his reason:
But thou wouldst teach him how to find
A shelter under every wind;
A hope for times that are unkind
 And every season.

WILLIAM WORDSWORTH

The Daisy scattered on each mead and down,
A golden tuft within a silver crown.

THOMAS BROWNE

# May
## HAWTHORNE
*symbol of hope*

The hawthorn bush with seats beneath the shade,
For talking age and whispering lovers made.

OLIVER GOLDSMITH

And every shepherd tells his tale
Under the hawthorne in the dale.

JOHN MILTON

Gives not the hawthorn bush a sweeter shade
To shepherds, looking on their silly sheep,
Than doth a rich embroider'd canopy
To kings that fear their subjects' treachery?

WILLIAM SHAKESPEARE

Yet walk with me where hawthorns hide
The wonders of the lane.

EBENEZER ELLIOTT

# June
## ROSE

According to the ancient Fable, the red colour of the Rose m be traced to Venus, whose delicate foot, when she was hasteni to the relief of her beloved Adonis, was pierced by a thorn, th drew blood.

L.E.

What's in a name? that which we call a rose
By any other name would smell as sweet.

WILLIAM SHAKESPEARE

The rose looks fair, but fairer we it deem
For that sweet odour that doth in it live.

WILLIAM SHAKESPEARE

Gather ye Rose-buds while ye may,
Old Time is still a-flying;
And this same flower that smiles today,
Tomorrow will be dying.

ROBERT HERRICK

"June brought Roses dripping with dew..."

# July
## PANSY

The pansy and the violet here
As seeming to descend
Both from one root and very fair
For sweetness yet contend.

MICHAEL DRAYTON

The pansy was exchanged between lovers—and thus was called: Love-in-idleness, Heartease, Kiss-me-at-the-garden-gate. The pansy was thought to inspire love; thus, in "Midsummer Night's Dream", Oberon tells Puck to place a Pansy on the eyes of Titania, so that, upon waking, she may fall in love with the first person she sees.

The beauteous pansies rise
In purple, gold and blue,
With tints of rainbow hues
Mocking the sunset skies.

THOMAS J. OUSELEY

Pray, love, remember: and there is pansies, that's for thoughts.

WILLIAM SHAKESPEARE

# August
## POPPY

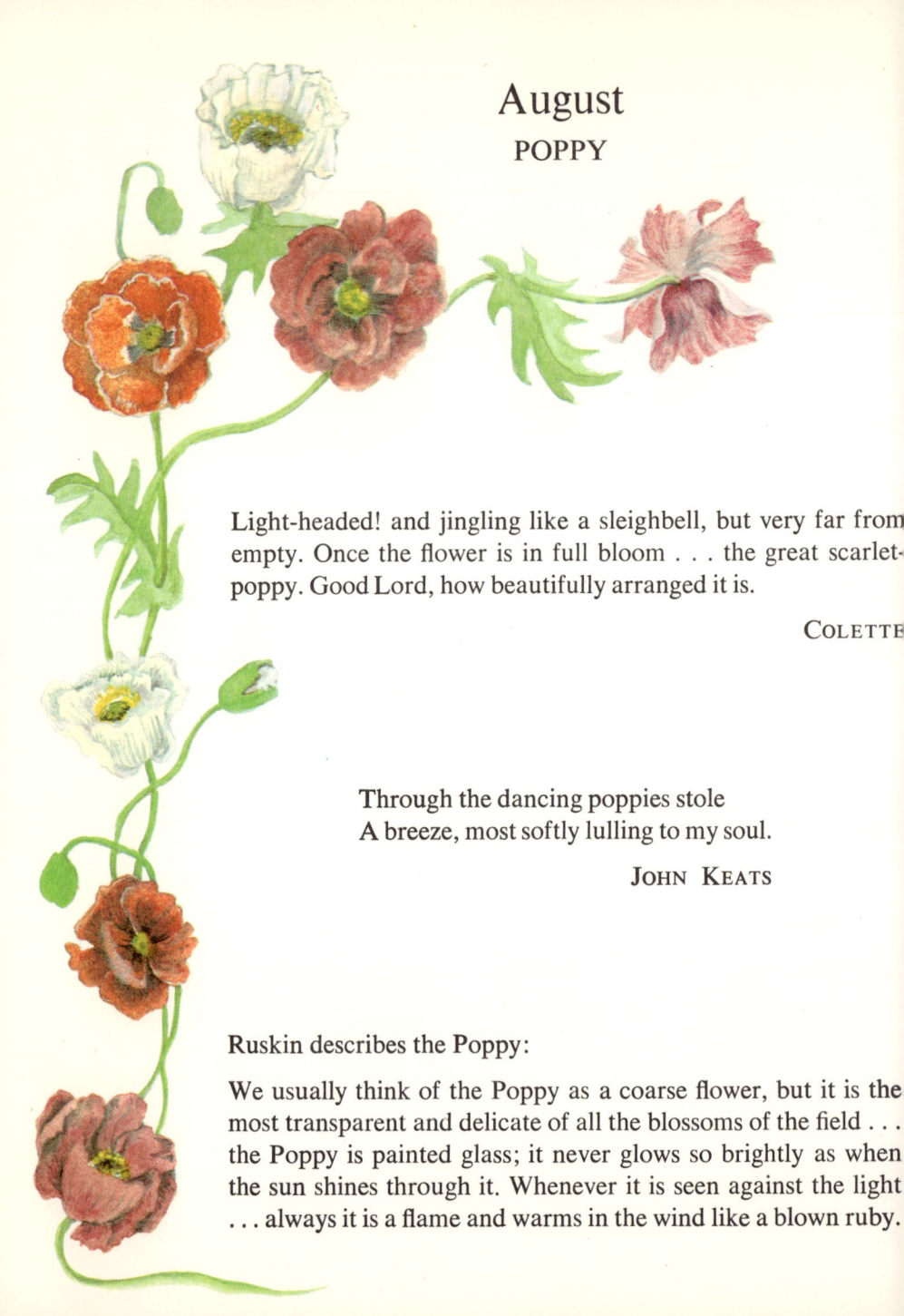

Light-headed! and jingling like a sleighbell, but very far from empty. Once the flower is in full bloom . . . the great scarlet-poppy. Good Lord, how beautifully arranged it is.

COLETTE

Through the dancing poppies stole
A breeze, most softly lulling to my soul.

JOHN KEATS

Ruskin describes the Poppy:

We usually think of the Poppy as a coarse flower, but it is the most transparent and delicate of all the blossoms of the field . . . the Poppy is painted glass; it never glows so brightly as when the sun shines through it. Whenever it is seen against the light . . . always it is a flame and warms in the wind like a blown ruby.

Poppies for dreams...
WILLIAM SHAKESPEARE

# September

## ASTER or "STARWORT"
*Emblem of after-thought*

The Aster begins to blow when other flowers are scarce. It is like an after-thought of Flora's, who smiles at leaving us.

L.E.L.

Chide me not, laborious band!
For the idle flowers I brought
Every aster in my hand
Goes home loaded with a thought.

RALPH WALDO EMERSON

Thou gazest on the stars:
Would I might be,
O star of mine, the skies
With myriad eyes
To gaze on thee.

ANONYMOUS

Brilliant and majestic, the Aster does not pretend to rival the rose, but it succeeds her, and consoles us in autumn for her absence.

                                                                      L.E.L.

# October
## CALENDULA, Commonly known as "MARIGOLD"

. . . the emblem of constancy in affection, and sympathy in joy and sorrow.

. . . this plant received the name "Calendula" because it was in flower on the calends of nearly every month. It has been called Marigold for a similar reason . . . the word gold having reference to its golden rays, likened to the rays of light around the head of the Blessed Virgin.

T. FORSTER

*The same is said by Lyte:*

The Marigold hath pleasant, bright and shining yellow flowers, the which do close at the setting down of the Sun and so spread open again at the Sun rising.

The wild Marsh Marigold shines like fire in swamps and hollows gray.

ALFRED LORD TENNYSON

# November
## CHRYSANTHEMUM

Bravest of brave sweet blossoms in all of the garden row;
Fair, when most of the flowers shrink from the winds
        that blow;
Gay, when the dismal North wind wails thru the tree-
        tops dumb;
Breathing a breath of gladness is the brave chrysanthemum.
One is of tawny color; another of cardinal glow,
As the cheek of a sun-warmed maiden and the reddest of
        wine will show;
While some are of gorgeous yellow, like gold in a
        monarch's crown,
And some of a royal purple, dusted with softest down.
Some of a creamy whitness, touched to a rosy blush,
As the snow of the lovely Jungfrau glows with a sunset
        flush;
Some flame at the heart, pearl petaled; and lavendar hued
        are some;
Yet each of them, crude or cultured, just a brave
        Chrysanthemum.

                              M. M. DODGE

Coming at the ripeness of the year, it symbolizes human perfection.

# December

## HOLLY

*The emblem of foresight.*

The Holly is an ornament to our woods, stripped bare by winter: its berries serve for food to the birds that never leave us, and its foliage affords them an hospitable shelter during the cold season. Thus, Nature, by a kind forethought, has taken care to preserve the verdure of this handsome tree all the year round, and to arm it with thorns, that it may furnish both food and protection to the innocent creatures which resort to it for refuge.

The Holly with its scarlet berries is the most beautiful of the evergreens that have been used for ages to adorn churches and houses at Christmas:

> With Holly and ivy
> So green and so gay,
> We deck up our houses
> As fresh as the day
> With bays and rosemary,
> And laurel complete,
> And every one now
> Is a king in conceit.
>
> L. E. L.

the Holly that outdares cold winter's ire
		Thomas Browne

*Honeysuckle,* the emblem of firm and fast affection — as it climbs round any tree or bush that is near it, clinging so tight as to leave its mark in deep furrows on the tree that supported it.

To gild refined gold, to paint the lily,
To throw perfume on the violet,
To smooth the ice, or add another hue
Unto the rainbow, or with taper light
To seek the beauteous eye of heaven to garnish
Is wasteful and ridiculous excess.

　　　　　　　WILLIAM SHAKESPEARE

And O and O
The daisies blow,
And the primroses are waken'd,
And the violets white,
Sit in silver plight,
And the green bud's as long as the spike end

　　　　　　　JOHN KEATS

Not a tree, a plant, a leaf, a blossom but contains a folio volume. We may read, and read, and read again, and still find something new, something to please, and something to instruct, e'en in the noisome weed.

JAMES HURDIS

A thing of beauty is a joy forever:
Its loveliness increases; it will never
Pass into nothingness; but still will keep
A bower quiet for us, and a sleep
Full of sweet dreams and health, and quiet breathing.

JOHN KEATS

Not a flower
But shows some touch, in freckle, streak, or stain
Of His unrivall'd pencil. He inspires
Their balmy odors, and imparts their hues,
And bathes their eyes with nectar, and includes
In grains as countless as the sea-side sands,
The forms with which He sprinkles all the earth.

WILLIAM COWPER

God made the flowers to beautify
The earth and cheer man's careful mood,
And he is happiest who hath power
To gather wisdom from a flower,
And wake his heart in every hour
To pleasant gratitude.

WILLIAM WORDSWORTH

Thick on the woodland floor
Gay company shall be,
Primrose and Hyacinth
And frail Anemone,
Perennial Strawberry-bloom
Woodsorrel's pencilled veil,
Dishevel'd Willow-Weed
And Orchids purple and pale.

        ROBERT BRIDGES

The twining jasmine and blushing rose
With lavish grace their morning scents disclose;
The smelling tube rose and jonquil declare
The stronger impulse of an evening air.

        MATTHEW PRIOR

The Cowslip is a country wench;
The Violet is a nun;
But I will woo the dainty Rose
The queen of everyone.

        THOMAS HOOD

*Tulip:* Yet, come closer, tulip that I wish to describe, come and keep me company. Come painted like an Easter egg, with a lick of orange and yellow . . . In your battalions you make a splash of splendor in the flat, water-steeped, assiduous landscape of the Netherlands . . . But come time of famine, and your precious bulbs were cooked and eaten . . .

                                              Colette

The Lily, lady of the flow'ring field.

        Edmund Spenser

These few pale autumn flowers
How beautiful they are!
Than all that went before
Than all the summer store,
How lovelier far!

                Anonymous

The Rose
Blendeth its odour with the violet, —
Solution sweet.

JOHN KEATS


The gentle flowers
Retired, and stooping over the wilderness,
Talked of humility, and peace and love.

ROBERT POLLOK


Forget-me-not — the blue bell — and
that Queen
Of secrecy, the violet.

JOHN KEATS


When daisies pied and violets blue
And lady-smocks all silver-white
And cuckoo birds of yellow hue
Do paint the meadows with delight.

WILLIAM SHAKESPEARE

How much there is of the heart's eloquence
In but a simple flower! — oh, flowers were made
For love's interpreters!

                L.E.L.


"Soon will the high midsummer pomp come on
Soon will the musk carnations break and swell,
Soon shall we have gold-dusted Snapdragon
Sweet-William with his homely cottage smell,
And stocks in fragrant blow . . .

            MATTHEW ARNOLD

Each beauteous flower,
Iris all hues, Roses and Jessamin
Rear'd high their flourish't heads between, and wrought
Mosaic; underfoot the violet,
Crocus and Hyacinth with rich inlay
Broider'd the ground, more coloured than with stone
Of costliest emblem.

            JOHN MILTON

Now blooms the Lily by the bank,
The primrose down the brae;
The hawthorne's budding in the glen,
And milkwhite is the slae.

    MARY, QUEEN OF SCOTS

To create a flower is the labour of ages.

    WILLIAM BLAKE

On many harps, which he has lately strung;
And when again your dewiness he kisses
Tell him I have you in my world of blisses!
So happily when I rove in some far vale
His might voice may come upon the gale.

    JOHN KEATS

Then came the cowslip
Like a dancer in the fair,
She spread her litle mat of green
And on it danced she,
With a fillet bound about her brow,
A fillet round her happy brow,
A golden fillet round her brow,
And rubies in her hair.

    SYDNEY DOBELL

Earth laughs in flowers.
RALPH WALDO EMERSON


The flower of sweetest smell is shy and lowly.
    WILLIAM WORDSWORTH

In youth from rock to rock I went,
From hill to hill in discontent
Of pleasure high and turbulent
Most pleased when most uneasy;
But now my own delights I make, —
My thirst at every rill can slake,
And gladly Nature's love partake
Of thee, sweet Daisy!

Thee winter in the garland wears
That thinly decks his few grey hairs;
Spring parts the clouds with softest airs,
That she may sun thee;
Whole summer-fields are thine by right;
And autumn, melancholy wight!
Doth in thy crimson head delight
When rains are on thee.

... Child of the Year! that round doth run
Thy course, bold lover of the sun,
And cheerful when the day's begun
As lark or leveret,
Thy long-lost praise thou shall regain;
Nor be less dear to future men
Than in old time; — thou not in vain
Art Nature's favorite.

WILLIAM WORDSWORTH